# CRITICAL ESSAYS IN MODERN LITERATURE

# Critical Essays in Modern Literature

# THE FICTION OF
# J. D. SALINGER

Frederick L. Gwynn
and
Joseph L. Blotner

UNIVERSITY OF PITTSBURGH PRESS

# Acknowledgments

This study doubtless owes something to the articles listed in the Bibliography, although it makes no conscious use of them, and was indeed conceived and shaped before most of them were published.

For a stimulus to re-assess "De Daumier-Smith's Blue Period," we are indebted to an unpublished essay by Eugene Goodheart, "The Remarkable Mr. Salinger." Our real obligation is to the following teachers and students who made helpful comments in the course of discussing Salinger's fiction or of going over the manuscript: Professors Eric Carlson, James R. Frakes, James E. Miller, Jr., Charles Murrah, William S. Weedon, Charles Weis, and Agnes L. Starrett, Director of the University of Pittsburgh Press; Messrs. E. T. DeJarnette, Jr. and Daniel F. McGrath; and students in the American Literature courses at the University of Virginia, 1955-1958.

Frederick L. Gwynn
*Trinity College, Connecticut*

Joseph L. Blotner
*University of Virginia*

# Contents

*The Fiction of*
*J. D. Salinger*

# I. INTRODUCTION

For the future historian, the most significant fact about American literary culture of the Post-War Period may be that whereas young readers of the Inter-War Period knew intimately the work of a goodly number of coeval writers (Hemingway, Fitzgerald, Dos Passos, Wolfe, Sinclair Lewis, for example), the only Post-War fiction unanimously approved by contemporary literate American youth consists of about five hundred pages by Jerome David Salinger.

Just why he is the one writer to whom so many young men and women, high-brow and middle-brow, in college and out, are devoted is not yet clear, although there is no lack of critical guesses as to the magnetic core of his work. For Heiserman and Miller (see Bibliography for these references), Salinger's fiction centers on the necessity for love, and its most striking feature is the poignancy of its humor. For David Stevenson, the typical crisis of a Salinger story sends the reader back into his own problems, making him aware of how we are "members all of the lonely crowd." Ihab Hassan sees a double conflict at the heart of Salinger's writing—the struggle between what Leslie Fiedler calls the "dream of innocence and the fact of guilt," and the tension between "the Assertive Vulgarian and the Responsive Outsider," the typical Salingerian hero being the outsider who expresses his responsiveness in a "strange quixotic gesture." Donald Barr feels that most of Salinger's fiction "is about those who think they are in hell." For William Wiegand, Salinger has not only revived the dialectal charm of Mark Twain, but like Thomas Mann has given us a coherent vision of the non-conformist who resists the disease of Illusion. To Maxwell Geismar, Salinger also speaks for non-conformism—that of the "Ivy League Rebellion of the Fifties" (Geismar does not tell us just what this is), but in the last analysis Salinger seems to Geismar to be perhaps the cleverest of the *New Yorker* Impressionist writers, whose staple theme is the lost innocence of childhood.

To all this we may add that if one labels Post-War youth the Beat Generation, one may see the fondness for Salinger as a literary retreat from the largeness and rhetoric paraded in current revivals of giants like Melville, James, and Faulkner; for Salinger's protagonists are mostly metropolitan introverts with whom the young reader can more easily identify himself than with, say, the aspiring Captain Ahab, Isabel Archer, or Thomas Sutpen. If one considers the Beat Generation "basically a religious generation"—as one of its spokesmen, Jack Kerouac, asseverates—and if "Beat means beatitude, not beat up,"[1] then one can conjecture about the relationship between Salinger's popularity and the fact that he is probably the only American writer of fiction ever to express a devotional attitude toward religious experience by means of a consistently satiric style. Or if one feels simply that the essence of sensitive youth is the impulsiveness of its explorations and retreats expressing itself in a mixture of unconscious idealism and self-conscious but humorous cynicism, then one has some notion of why there is a gap left by Nelson Algren, Kingsley Amis, Samuel Beckett, Truman Capote, Ralph Ellison, James Jones, Wright Morris, and Tennessee Williams (to mention a few contemporary and various originals)—a gap that is filled by J. D. Salinger.

Finally — and most importantly for us — one may feel that a half-dozen of Salinger's short pieces of fiction are nearly perfectly organized works, with a variety of organizations, in which vivid human characters are involved in the basic human conflict between love and what Salinger's Esmé calls squalor—that is, evil, trouble, inhumanity, and sin—and in which the characters and conflict are embodied in original and memorable symbols that are often humorous, even as the dialogue and narration are always humorous.

To be able to make this assertion, however, requires an examination of the *corpus* of Salinger's work: one novel, two short novels, and thirty short stories, published over a period of almost two decades. The present study, which considers each piece of fiction on its own merits, comes to the early conclusion that Salinger's achievement, described in the paragraph above, occurs in what may currently be called the middle of his career, and that the progress of his creativity has run up from second-rate magazine items to the half-dozen masterworks, and thence downward, most recently, to ambitious failures.

This examination has little concern with the author himself, for two reasons. In the first place, we are chiefly interested in discovering specific elements in each work that contribute to the success or failure of the work, and in noting the incidence of these elements in the comparative progress of Salinger's art; we do not propose specu-

3

lating as to how this author's life and work have dove-tailed with each other. Secondly, even if we wanted to see the author in his fiction, we would have a difficult job in acquiring much to see with. An apparently secretive man, Salinger has revealed to the public (chiefly via magazine editors and in *Twentieth Century Authors: First Supplement*) only that he was born in New York City in 1919 and brought up there, that he went to public school, to a Pennsylvania military academy, and to three colleges without a degree; that he traveled in Europe before the War, and during the War —when, as a staff sergeant in the Fourth Infantry Division, he took part in five combat campaigns from D-Day to V-E Day. Beyond this, and the record of his publications registered in the Bibliography, almost everything about this popular writer is unknown to the public.

## 1. The High Point of Salinger's Art:
"For Esmé—With Love and Squalor"

At the outset, it might be well to consider Salinger's major fictional victory—the victories being the only reason for considering any of the failures that punctuate his unique career. The high point of his art, the moment at which particular narrative and general truth are identified most successfully with one another, comes in his most famous story, "For Esmé—With Love and Squalor," when Sergeant X, stationed in Bavaria after V-E Day, reads a German inscription in a German book and caps it with a Russian quotation written in English. The four agents in this process are perfectly chosen, and three of them are presented simply and at top speed. The reader is told that the book is *Die Zeit ohne Beispiel* by

Joseph Goebbels, that one inscription is by a 38-year-old unmarried woman, "a low official in the Nazi Party," and that the other inscription is from Dostoevsky. The fourth agent, Sergeant X, whose gesture of quotation sounds the depths of the human condition, thereby prepares himself and the reader for the salvation he receives from someone else's gesture later in the story.

What Goebbels represents should be obvious to anyone over thirty, but surely the range of this evil can not be fully registered on the generation that adores Salinger, and it may even have dimmed in the more timeworn mind. To make any kind of contact with Joseph Goebbels is to be overwhelmed by the very type of psychotic hatred for everything weaker or more human than itself. His diaries show him to be "the unflagging motive force behind the vicious anti-Semitism of the Nazi regime," as Hugh Gibson says, whose "aim was the extermination of all Jews"; an ex-Catholic, he planned to "deal with the churches after the war and reduce them to impotence." It was this man, the holder of a *bona fide* doctorate, who in 1933 personally selected and had burned thousands of printed pages in which man had communicated with man. Less known than the genocide and the book-burning is Goebbel's hatred for humanity itself. In 1925 he wrote in his diary: "I have learned to despise the human being from the bottom of my soul. He makes me sick in my stomach." A year later he concluded that "The human being is a *canaille*."

But as Louis Lochner says, "Nobody who has not lived under Nazism can grasp how absolute was Goebbels's control of the German mind." It is this irresistible influence that (we may guess) had stimulated the second agent in the Salinger situation first to her Nazi Party activities and later to the revulsion that she expressed by penning in the Goebbels book that X finds:

" 'Dear God, life is hell.' " To X, "the words appeared to have the stature of an uncontestable, even classic indictment," and he impulsively writes a comment underneath, one of Father Zossima's exhortations in *The Brothers Karamazov*: " 'Fathers and teachers, I ponder 'What is hell?' I maintain that it is the suffering of being unable to love.' "

The woman's substitution of the Christian God for Hitler and Goebbels is paralleled by the Sergeant's reference to Russian Christianity, and her implicit recognition of *Die Zeit ohne Beispiel*— The Unprecedented Era—as unprecedented hell is paralleled by Zossima's and X's awareness of the non-love that brings about disintegration and war; together these form not only a "classic indictment" but a profound objective correlative for the love and "squalor" experienced by Sergeant X—and the reader—in the rest of the story. (It is the young girl Esmé who asks Sergeant X to write her an "extremely squalid and moving" story, adding the question, " 'Are you at all acquainted with squalor?' " The Sergeant's answer is typically ironic but correct: "I said not exactly but that I was getting better acquainted with it, in one form or another, all the time. . . .") We may now see exactly what is correlated.

The conflict of "Esmé" places the protagonist, Sergeant X, against four "squalid" forces in the four chronological sections of the story. (1) In 1950, the present, he is set off against his wife, "a breathtakingly levelheaded girl," and his mother-in-law. (2) Back in April 1944, he is set off against the dullness of pre-Invasion training and the in-

6

communicativeness of his sixty male mates, as well as against his wife and his mother-in-law, the women who write selfish civilian letters to this soldier about to be landed in France. (3) In the long year from D-Day in 1944 to V-E-Day in 1945 (referred to only briefly in the story), the protagonist is set off against war itself (which has resulted in his nervous breakdown) as well as against his jeep-mate, Corporal Clay. (4) In May 1945, Sergeant X's combat fatigue is set off against the insensitivity of the loutish Clay, as well as against the selfish civilian triviality of his brother (who writes asking for souvenirs) and Clay's girl Loretta (who sits at home callously and amateurishly derogating X's psyche).

To balance these "squalid" antagonists there are four demonstrations of "love." (1) In 1950, exactly six years after X met Esmé, and apparently without any communication between them during this period, he receives an invitation to her wedding that makes him want to fly to it, "expenses be hanged." (2) In 1944, he has met Esmé, a brave English orphan of thirteen, who, nervous like X ("her nails were bitten down to the quick," "her hand, as I'd suspected, was a nervous hand, damp at the palm"), is also precociously sensitive to artistic, intellectual, and emotional values. (3) Set opposite X's shattering experience in the war against Germany is the simple inscription in the book that communicates to him the shattering experience of a German in the war against the Allies. In answering the *cri de coeur* of an enemy whom he has actually just arrested as a criminal, Sergeant X equates himself with her simply as human beings against the total war they have suffered in— "a method of existence that is ridiculous to say the least," as Esmé naively but perceptively describes

7

World War II. (4) Finally, in 1945, X receives the wrist watch which Esmé mailed to him the day after D-Day, almost a year before. It is a stunning gesture for a titled gentlewoman who is "Usually not terribly gregarious" thus to give her father's watch to a G. I., a foreigner casually and briefly met, a man who had countered almost every one of her statements with an ironic answer. The gift, which belonged to a British nobleman "s-l-a-i-n" in war (in her younger brother's hearing she spells out crucial words), helps restore the possibility of life ("f-a-c-u-l-t-i-e-s") for the American Staff Sergeant X.

## II.  THE LONG DEBUT:

### *The Apprentice Period (1940-1948)*

This perfectly realized tale of love and war is the artistic apex of a classic period, 1948-1951, in which six stories and the novel *The Catcher in the Rye* were published. It was not always thus. Before finishing this period, Salinger had printed twenty tales notably absent from his only collection, *Nine Stories*. Most of them were commercial stories that appeared in *Collier's*, *The Saturday Evening Post*, and *Cosmopolitan;* but four of them were more arty sketches published in *Story,* whose editor, Whit Burnett, had taught Salinger short-story writing at Columbia and ushered him into print in the spring of 1940. And a half-dozen of them introduced sympathetic characters who—under the influence of the same World War experience that the writer underwent—develop attitudes and relationships and names that end in the fruitful Caulfield and Glass families with whom Salinger is later to feel so much at home. To change classifications, one may note that three of the apprentice works can be written off as short short stories, four as somewhat conventional tales of the Lonely Girl, three as Destroyed Artist melodramas, and three as Marriage in Wartime stories. Another six are worth more consideration.

## 1. The Short Short Stories

The short shorts consist of two of the genuine *Collier's* surprise-ending pieces and one satire of this type in *Esquire*. (1) In "The Hang of It" tough Sergeant Grogan gives up on bumbling Private Pettit, just as he had given up in 1917 on Private Pettit, the boy's father—now *Colonel* Pettit of the regiment. (2) "Personal Notes on an Infantryman" simply reverses this military and family relationship. Lieutenant Lawlor tries to discourage an overage private who insists on making good and turning out to be the Lieutenant's father. (3) *Esquire* printed "The Heart of a Broken Story" as Satire rather than Fiction, since it begins with a Boy about to fall for a Girl he sees on a bus, proceeds to fantasies on how to have Boy meet Girl, and ends with Boy taking up with Other Girl, First Girl having been in love with Other Boy all the time. "And that's why I never wrote a boy-meets-girl story for *Collier's*," Salinger concludes. "In a boy-meets-girl story the boy should always meet the girl." Not a very promising start for a writer whose stories would sell a million and a quarter copies.

## 2. The Lonely Girl Characterizations

Three of the four Lonely Girl tales appeared in *Story* and one in *Mademoiselle*. (1) "The Young Folks," Salinger's first publication, is better done than the others, and indeed, better than anything up to "Once a Week Won't Kill You" four years later. Wallflower Edna, whose pathetic chatter and insinuations are skillfully rendered, fails to impress stupid Bill at a college kids' party, but after retiring, presumably to cry, she reappears to

10

pretend that she's still part of the gaiety. (2) "The Long Debut of Lois Taggett" recounts how long it takes a strange New York debutante (Lois says "ya" and "wanna") to grow up, the process requiring one marriage to a sadist and one to a boor, maternity, and the death of the baby. The story's end offers the signal of Lois's maturity: she stops nagging her husband for wearing white socks. (3) "Elaine" represents so marked a regression as almost to suggest that the artist had been reading James T. Farrell a decade too late. Elaine Cooney is a beautiful moron of sixteen, brought up on movies and radio by a moronic mother who whisks her daughter home from her wedding to a movie usher. That's all. (4) "A Young Girl in 1941 with No Waist at All" is Barbara, a slow-thinking but pleasant 18-year-old who finds a new young man proposing to her on a cruise she is taking with her future mother-in-law. Upset by the new proposal but not understanding why, she tells Mrs. Odenhearn that she does not want to get married— much to the latter's relief. The Chorus of the story, the ebullient Mrs. Woodruff, mourns the difficulties in store for the war youth of 1941, and Barbara's situation may be meant as a case in point, but the writer's last words identify Barbara's unresolved crisis merely with "the last minute of her girlhood."

### 3. The Destroyed Artist Melodramas

Better than any other sequence, the Destroyed Artist trio of stories shows a Salinger struggling with a theme he wants to be able to handle but which he really does not seem to understand. With "The Varioni Brothers," "The Inverted Forest," and "Blue Melody," Salinger never decides who

11

the protagonist really is, what the central conflict really is, or whether or not any of the conflicts really make any difference to any of the possible protagonists.

(1.) For example, whose story is "The Varioni Brothers"? Is it about Joe Varioni, who fails to finish a wonderful novel because he must write lyrics for brother Sonny's popular songs? Or is it about Sonny, the heel who comes to appreciate Joe's work a dozen years after his sacrificial death? Or could it possibly be about Sarah Daley Smith, from whose point of view the story is told and who understands both the destroyed genius and the reformed heel? Even if the reader chooses, he is reluctant to believe that any one of these persons would ever be mixed up with the others, anyway.

(2.) "The Inverted Forest," a short novel (24-000 words) complete in one issue of *Cosmopolitan*, is so far from the Salinger of the only other novel, *The Catcher in the Rye*, that its irredeemably fantastic plot should be summarized. In 1918 Corinne von Nordhoffen, 11-year-old daughter of a German baron and an heiress who committed suicide, is having a birthday party on Long Island. Unhappy because her favorite, a poor boy named Raymond Ford, does not attend, she goes to look for him only to see him being pulled out of town by his tough mother, a waitress. After the Baron dies, Corinne goes to Wellesley and becomes six feet tall. She then spends three years in Europe, liking only a young man who is killed by falling from the running-board of her car. Back in New York, she occasionally sees Robert Waner—the narrator of the story up to a point—who loved her unsuccessfully in college, got her a job on a news-magazine, and watched her rise to be its drama critic.

On Corinne's thirtieth birthday, Waner gives her a book of poems by Ray Ford, now a known poet and an instructor at Columbia. She loves the verse, especially the lines "Not wasteland, but a great inverted forest/with all foliage underground" (indeed, the best lines in the story), and she uncovers their creator. In ten weeks of talking-dates in Chinese restaurants, she gets Ray's life story from him. His mother was alcoholic, and he has never taken a drink or smoked or been in love; he worked in Florida at a racetrack until rescued by a Mrs. Rizzio, who let him use her library and educate himself. Soon Corinne and Ray are married, despite Waner's warning that Ray cannot really love her and that he is "the most gigantic psychotic you'll ever know."

After the honeymoon, Bunny Croft, a literary college girl, enters their lives. (Somewhere in here, Salinger and Waner give up the chore of narration by means of an improbable note from Corinne stating that she will tell the rest of the story in the form of a private detective's log.) Soon Corinne drinks, Ray drinks, and Ray and Bunny run off from New York together. Corinne is consoled and upset by oafish Howie Croft, who, married to Bunny for ten years, reveals her as a shallow, adulterous, and alcoholic monster rather than the esthetic *aficionada* she seemed. Eighteen months later, Corinne finds Ray and Bunny in a mid-Western slum, where Ray sits drunkenly pushing papers around a card table in a pathetic attempt at self-deception and Bunny "works" on her twelfth "book." Ray explains to Corinne that he can't escape because he is "with the Brain again.... *You* saw the original. Think back. Think of somebody pounding on the window of a restaurant on a dark street. *You* know the one I mean"—presum-

13

ably his own crude mother who has passed alcoholism on to him. The End.

Once again, does all this happen to Corinne or to Ford—or even to Waner? (Surely Bunny is just an agent.) And what *is* significant about what *has* happened? It is that Corinne has failed to grow up, that Ford has succumbed to a mother-image, or even that Waner has been the Jamesian observer who turns out to have lost all by observing? If we care, we can only note finally that the worst things happen to Ray Ford and that it is his forest that is inverted. But the immediate corollary to this is that we have never been able to see this submerged forest for the mass of roots crawling about on the surface.

(3.) Finally, there is the *Cosmopolitan* Blue Ribbon story, "Blue Melody," another case of triple schizophrenia. Plainly the story wants to be about Lida Jones, a Negro blues singer who (in a situation based on accounts of the tragic end of Bessie Smith) dies from appendicitis because the Southern white hospitals to which she is taken will not admit her. But Lida's story is witnessed and told by a white boy named Rudford, who appreciated blues when he was nine years old, and who taught Peggy Moore to love jazz and him when they were kids, even though she gets married and materialistic a dozen years later. But this is not all. The narrator of the story is not Rudford but *another* person, a man who hears the tale of Rudford and Lida in an Army truck in Germany in World War II, who inserts a note of admiration for Lida's records, and who then promptly disappears from the reader's ken.

14

## 4. The Marriage in Wartime Group

The next three tales, all published in 1944 while the author was undergoing the experiences in the European Theatre of Operations that would produce "For Esmé," are polarized between two commercials in *The Saturday Evening Post* and one impressionistic fiction in *Story*.

(1.) "Both Parties Concerned" are Billy and Ruth, both under twenty when they married, he now bored by war plant work and fatherhood, she worried by his need for diversion. Ruth goes home to mother but returns when Billy becomes understanding and responsible.

(2.) The "Soft-Boiled Sergeant," Burns, is soft-boiled not about his wife and her love of sentimental war movies but about her appreciation of his appreciation of Sergeant Burke, who befriended the boy rookie Burns in 1922 and who was killed at Pearl Harbor trying to save three buck privates.

(3.) "Once a Week Won't Kill You" is what Richard, leaving for war, says to his wife Virginia as he urges her to take his dotty Aunt Rena to the movies while he's gone. This story could have been good: the reader can feel empathetically for the husband in his predicament and the wife in her dilemma, and he can relish the pathos of Aunt Rena's disoriented but noble response to Richard's departure. But the tale is unhappily split into two separate scenes, with Virginia and Aunt Rena never engaged in the dialogue that would have made the differences between them truly poignant. And there are mysterious unexploited references to Richard's mother, who may have drowned with his father in a sailing accident; but

Salinger fails to make plain the analogy (if he means it at all) between the mother who used to whistle "I Can't Behave on Sundays 'Cause I'm Bad Seven Days a Week" and the wife who starts to be bad about taking Aunt Rena to the movies *once* a week. All in all, the most that can be said for these three Husband vs. Wife in Wartime stories is that they point up the same theme's minor embodiment in "A Perfect Day for Bananafish" and "For Esmé."

## 5. The Caulfield Stories

The most interesting of the early sequences is the sextet of stories that do develop five years later into "For Esmé," "Bananafish," and *The Catcher in the Rye*. (1.) On "The Last Day of the Last Furlough" before going overseas, Sergeant Babe Gladwaller is home reading Tolstoy, Dostoevsky, and Scott Fitzgerald (he incidentally mentions the Father Zossima whom another sergeant was to quote so movingly). Salinger himself may have been reading Ernest Hemingway's story "Soldier's Home," for Babe, like Harold Krebs, soon gets involved in keeping his destination secret from his mother and in talking with his ten-year-old sister, Mattie—who understands him much as Phoebe Caulfield does Holden in the novel. Babe has two personal problems outside his family—his love for the disdainful Frances, and his friendship with the cynical Vincent Caulfield, son of an actor and himself a writer of soap operas, whose brother Holden has once again run away from school.

(2.) "A Boy in France" is Babe again, digging into a foxhole and reading "for the thirty-oddth time" a loving letter from his sister containing news of the haughty Frances. Like Esmé's letter to Sergeant X and Zooey Glass's phone-call to his sister Franny in "Zooey," the communication relaxes him and he falls asleep.

(3.) But "This Sandwich Has No Mayonnaise" shifts to Vincent Caulfield, now seen training in Georgia in the Air Corps, trying to make G.I. conversation while distracted by the news that his 19-year-old brother Holden, who had got through the European war, is missing in action in the Pacific. Unfortunately for the unity of the tale, the interest shifts to Vincent's lieutenant, who graciously arranges for an 18-year-old private to go to a dance —a small sacrificial act that Vincent should have been made to perform if his feeling for Holden were to be rendered to us by more than wordy reminiscence.

(4.) Babe Gladwaller survives the war, but Vincent does not, and in "The Stranger" Babe takes *his* little sister Mattie to New York to tell Vincent's girl—now Mrs. Bob Polk—about Vincent's death in the Hürtgen Forest. Helen is the ideal Salinger girl, with records and books in her apartment (Fitzgerald again, and the Rilke whose work Seymour Glass's wife significantly avoids and his sister Franny espouses). But Helen did not marry Vincent because he was so cynical: "He didn't believe anything from the time little Kenneth Caulfield died. His brother." Now, if this report about Vincent is true, then the story is torpedoed by the very melodrama it seeks to avoid (seeks to avoid by having Mattie along, by having Helen happily married, and by getting nowhere). On the other hand, if we recall and utilize the cynical Vincent of "The Last Day of the Last Furlough," we lose out on the poignancy of Holden-Kenneth's death. And if we still feel keenly about Holden (because we see the relation between Babe and his own sister Mattie, and she's still alive), we are undercut on the poignancy of Vincent's death. Once again, the writer has not seen it through.

(5.) Yet three weeks after "The Stranger," *Collier's* also published "I'm Crazy," which concentrates on Holden at last, and indeed, is a reasonably complete sketch of the exodus and homecoming of Holden in *The Catcher in the Rye,* with the profane adolescent language omitted for the sake of a family readership. (6.) A year later, Salinger entered *The New Yorker* for the first time with the wonderful Holden-Sally Hayes episode in Rockefeller Center, called here "Slight Rebellion off Madison," which once again avoided the vulgar phrasing that in *Catcher* allows Holden's climactic opinion of Sally to stamp him as at once neurotic, self-reliant, and honest. We are now in the realm of Salinger's great success, and it is dispiriting to note that even a year after this story he could print "The Inverted Forest" in *Cosmopolitan.* Not to mention "A Girl I Knew," a rambling picaresque tale apparently based on the writer's own abortive career as a trainee in a family meat-packing business in Europe in 1937. The comic aspect of an 18-year-old American Werther psychoanalyzed in Vienna is delightful, but it hardly jibes with the climax—the narrator's return during World War II to find that his beautiful innocent Leah has been burned up in a Hitler incinerator. Even if Salinger is deliberately contrasting the two periods of his story, the second is simply too deep for tears, let alone for the parody style in which the first is presented.

But a month after "The Inverted Forest" came "A Perfect Day for Bananafish."

# III.  ALL HIS FACULTIES INTACT:

*The Classic Period (1948-1951)*

## 1. "A Perfect Day for Bananafish" (1948)

To turn to the period of Salinger's major esthetic successes is to enter a world of psychically under-privileged persons occasionally saved by love. Sicker than Holden Caulfield and Sergeant X, Seymour Glass of "A Perfect Day for Bananafish" is destroyed by his own hypersensitivity pathetically heightened by lack of love. Released from an Army hospital, he is unable to adjust to life with his crass wife Muriel amidst the lavish and vulgar atmosphere of their post-war second honeymoon, in the Miami Beach which Philip Wylie once called "the loveless tunnel of love." Oblivious to poetry but responsive to expensive clothes and tabloid-magazine sex, Muriel seems to be incapable of giving Seymour the love that will make him whole. The attention he does receive, from a four- or five-year-old child, serves ultimately only to reveal further to him the impossibility of his situation.

Everything is compact and organic in this story, despite its division into two separate scenes. The first part of the tale renders the characters of Muriel (to Seymour, "Miss Spiritual Tramp of 1948") and her mother and a part of Seymour's case history in one long telephone call; and the second part reveals Seymour's needs and emotional state in a scene culminating with his suicide. Salinger skillfully manipulates the images which suggest an underlying motif: Seymour's sexual inadequacy. There is his obsession with trees, his story of the engorged bananafish trapped in the banana hole, his paranoiac suspicion that a woman is staring critically at his bare feet, and his choice of the pistol as the suicide weapon. Like Holden Caulfield and Sergeant X, Seymour Glass (he sees more than others and he shatters like glass) forms his most satisfying relationship with a sexually immature female child, but this girl's fateful name is Sybil, and she prophetically *sees* not only a bananafish but a doomed one with six bananas in his mouth; earlier she has been concerned with the six tigers of *Little Black Sambo*, who, we may recall, destroyed themselves through gluttony and vanity. In the water he kisses the arch of her foot, which she has recently stuck "in a soggy, collapsed castle" of sand. She too suffers from lack of affection: her mother sends her off to play while she goes for a midday martini ("I'll bring you the olive"). And even Sybil's affection has its blemish —her jealousy of three and a half-year-old Sharon Lipschutz.

The situation and its meaning are reinforced, in part ironically, by a seemingly casual reference of Muriel's to a volume of German poems by a man Seymour had called *"the only great poet of the century."* This can only be Rainer Maria Rilke, the sensitive and frustrated spirit who, like Seymour, was unable to adjust to the military and to the bourgeois worlds, failed in his marriage, and was emotionally involved with young girls.[2]

Two other Salinger hallmarks are here—realistic dialogue and functional sarcasm—but the real success of "A Perfect Day for Bananafish" rests upon the way that the disturbed young man, deprived of love, recognizes symbolically the inevitability of his destruction. Yet unlike Sergeant X, whose suffering and compassion take him outside himself, Seymour's concerns succeed only in turning him wholly inward. For example, his quixotic gesture of kissing Sybil's foot seems to have only a personal and pathological rationale; if he had possessed an awareness of the compassion often seen in Dostoevskian characters such as the one Sergeant X remembers, Seymour's story might have been different. Indeed, one of the most universalizing gestures in *Crime and Punishment* comes when Raskolnikov kisses Sonia's foot and says, " 'I did not bow down to you, I bowed down to all the suffering of humanity' " (Garnett translation). Because Seymour Glass and Sybil Carpenter are so preoccupied with their own feet, the story falls below the heights of "For Esmé," but it still has a power beyond melodrama.

## 2. "Uncle Wiggily in Connecticut" (1948)

There is the same power in the next tale, published two months later in *The New Yorker*. Here the conflict lies in the degeneration of the young matron Eloise Wengler as her marital life is measured against her pre-marital life. Her earlier innocence, emotionality, and appreciation of tenderness and humor have been replaced by cynicism, insensitivity, and derision. All this is symbolized by the title's contrast between Uncle Wiggily, the kind old rabbit of the Howard Garis stories, and Connecticut, where the disappointments of suburban domesticity are alleviated only by alcohol and nostalgia. Eloise apparently came from Idaho. Eloise's nostalgia is chiefly for Walt, "the only boy I ever knew that could make me laugh," who patted her twisted ankle and said "Poor Uncle Wiggily" (Garis's rabbit was always complaining about his rheumatism), and who was killed in the Army, not in combat but in a freak accident that incidentally identifies him as Seymour Glass's brother. Eloise's husband is Walt's opposite—an unhumorous, jealous man (possibly both with good cause), whose favorite author is actually L. Manning Vines and not the Jane Austen he declared during courtship. ("Raise High the Roof Beam, Carpenters" tags *him* as probably having been Buddy Glass's Army company commander in 1942.)

All this would make a predictable *New Yorker* product were it not for the presence in the story of Eloise's daughter Ramona, a little girl who serves the functions of both dramatizing Eloise's degeneration and paralleling it. The dramatizing comes about in the impasse between mother and daughter: Eloise resents Ramona's looking like her father and grandmother, her childish scratching and picking, and most of all, her imaginary beau, Jimmy Jimmereeno. But Jimmy stands in the same relation to Ramona as Walt does to Eloise—a symbol of the secret image of love, unhampered by awful reality. Ramona characterizes Jimmy by green eyes, black hair, and no freckles (he is unique); by lacking parents (he can be monopolized); by a sword (he is a masculine, military hero). Walt is unique in his humor and tenderness, is not connected with having or being parents, and is an ironical military hero—in that altogether "he felt he was advancing in the Army, but in a different direction from everybody else" by being

22

about to *lose* insignia in each promotion; further-more, he was really killed while in the Army, and if Eloise should tell her husband Lou about it, "I'd tell him he was killed in action."

What brings together the motifs of Eloise's overt inhumanity and her secret innocent love is her sudden identification of herself with Ramona. To appreciate this climax, the reader must utilize a fact about Eloise almost concealed by Salinger —her unprepossessing face. "What I need is a cocker spaniel or something," she tells Mary Jane, the confidante of the story, "Somebody that looks like me." And to her home-coming husband, whom she callously leaves stranded at the station, she says: "I'm not funny. Really I'm not. It's just my face." This is Eloise's salvation, for it enables her to release her secret lost love into an active bond, albeit brief and drunken, with her myopic daughter, as she puts her to bed: "She picked up Ramona's glasses and, holding them in both hands, pressed them against her cheek. Tears rolled down her face, wetting the lenses. 'Poor Uncle Wiggily,'" she said over and over again. And at the very end, she sobs to Mary Jane: "'You remember our freshman year ... ? ... I was a nice girl, ... wasn't I?'"

This is remarkably well done, and we are touched, although we may feel that Eloise's salva-tion-by-child is as abrupt and as temporary as Seymour Glass's.

### 3. "Just Before the War with the Eskimos" (1948)

The final *New Yorker* story for that year drama-tizes the growth of an adolescent's human sym-pathy. Ginnie Mannox, 15, is normally nice and normally resentful of her stingy friend Selena

Graff, but she abrogates her demands for repayment from Selena after discovering the pathetic situation of Selena's 24-year-old misfit brother. Franklin Graff will not only not go back and finish college, but also he has been scorned by Ginnie's sister and is apparently now in the clutches of the mannered, effeminate Eric—one of Salinger's most successful caricatures, who talks in italics. More significantly, Franklin suffers from a paranoia aggravated by having been 4-F in World War II. "Look at 'em," he says of the crowds of New York humanity, "Goddam fools. . . . They're all goin' over to the goddam draft board. We're gonna fight the Eskimos next." Ginnie's answer—"*You* wouldn't have to go, anyway"—momentarily destroys any rapport between them. But it is Franklin who then forces on her half a sandwich, which (after meeting Eric and realizing the situation) she preserves in her pocket—a fetishistic gesture of sympathy for the pathetic Graff condition.

## 4. "The Laughing Man" (1949)

"The Laughing Man" of a year later is a complete change in theme and technique from the three previous *New Yorker* stories. Apparently simple, it turns out to be one of the most sophisticated and intricate of all of Salinger's tales. Humorous and perceptive in its insights into adolescent megalomania, it seemingly does little more than to juxtapose a fantastic story with a real-life romance. Actually, it is the recollection by a mature man of a crucial experience at the age of nine: the end of a hero-worship-laden relationship with an idealized older man who, preoccupied with his own romance, killed off the fictional projection of himself to which the boy had given unabashed

24

and imitative devotion.

John Gedsudski, former athlete and now N.Y.U. law student, is proprietor and "Chief" of the pre-teenage Comanche Club, to whom he tells a serialized extravagant story. The story—a great improvement over its ridiculous and distant source, Victor Hugo's *L'Homme Qui Rit* (1869)—relates the adventures of the heroic Laughing Man. Kidnaped from missionary parents by Chinese bandits, he is horribly disfigured by them. Growing up, his face concealed by a poppy-petal mask, he becomes an admired master criminal, the scourge of the Paris-China border, idolized by his faithful followers—Black Wing the timber wolf, Omba the dwarf, Hong the giant Mongolian, and a "gorgeous Eurasian girl."

The story takes on depth if one assumes that the Laughing Man is John Gedsudski's unconscious wish-fulfilling projection of himself. Just as Gedsudski is ugly, but a self-made success who is vastly admired by the boys, so the Laughing Man is ugly ("Strangers fainted dead away at the sight of the Laughing Man's horrible face"), but a self-made success (he has learned to speak with the animals and has "amassed the largest personal fortune in the world") who is vastly admired (by his "blindly loyal confederates").

Gedsudski's eidolon is in part a manifestation of the intrusion of an adult relationship into the idyllic adolescent one existing between the Chief and the Comanches. The Chief, a Staten Islander who wears a leather windbreaker and does not own gloves, is in love with Mary Hudson, who crosses the Long Island-Wellesley border into New York City and wears a beaver coat. One surmises that the differences in background between the two lovers (which Gedsudski symbolically combats through his creation of the Laughing Man and his Eurasian girl) are responsible for the breakup between the two which in turn precipitates the destruction of the old relationship between the Chief and the narrator. As the boy watches, the Chief is defeated: "Mary Hudson, she was over near third base crying. The Chief had hold of the sleeve of her beaver coat, but she got away from him. She ran off the field onto the cement path and kept running till I couldn't see her any more. The Chief didn't go after her. He just stood watching her disappear." It is then, on the way home in the bus, that Gedsudski curtly and inexplicably (to the Comanches) causes the Laughing Man to fail, too —the fictional agents of destruction being an "exquisite" daughter, and a father, the bitter enemy Marcel Dufarge, who kills the Laughing Man after finding "his daughter stretched out supine on the ground" as a result of seeing the Laughing Man's "naked face by moonlight"—the Chief's disguised fantasy of what Mr. Hudson's attitude toward his daughter's admirer must be. The effect upon the Comanches of the Laughing Man's agonizing death is traumatic. All are stunned into silence, one bursts into tears, and the narrator arrives home "with my teeth chattering uncontrollably."

After the brusque destruction of this image which the narrator, loving Gedsudski, had loved, things can never be the same. Salinger's sensitive handling of this complex of experience becomes more admirable with each reading of the story, for in it he has achieved a very difficult thing, even apart from the deft balancing of humor and poignancy: he has seemed to present from the point of view of sardonic recollection an experience of childhood fantasy in which adult concerns intruded without being recognized by the child, at the same time that he has presented an experience of adulthood symbolized in fantasy without being recognized by either child or adult.

## 5. "Down at the Dinghy" (1949)

As in all of Salinger's best work, a child is near the center of the story, but this time the writer has taken another step and gone beyond the familiar failure of personal love to a problem of social groups. Like the earlier Ramona Wengler and the later Teddy McArdle, Lionel Tannenbaum has an overactive interior life; but where they are the children of inadequately loving parents, he is a victim of external social hate in the form of anti-Semitism. And it is the jibe at his father by Sandra, the vindictive maid, which has made Lionel decide again to retreat, to run away from the home where he has been hurt. As one anticipates the woundings to come later in childhood, adolescence, and adulthood, it seems that the time of the story, Indian Summer, may be symbolic—the last of the kind of innocence which makes possible for him the semantic confusion at the end of the story. Two of Lionel's acts may also be symbolic. He rejects, throws overboard, two objects: a pair of underwater goggles (belonging to—of all people—his uncle, whom Sybil Carpenter had called See-more Glass) and a key chain with keys on it, objects from the adult world associated with his uncle and his father, both of whom presumably have met the problem posed in uglier terms than those in which he has met it through Sandra. There is a world of facts he unconsciously does not want to see, whose doors he does not want to open.

Another major aspect of this story is its implicit

suggestion of one reason for the problem of anti-Semitism—the failure of communication. As the story is divided into three parts, so the background of the problem is exemplified in three ways. There is of course no real understanding between Sandra and the Tannenbaums. Nor is there any between Sandra and the other servant, Mrs. Snell, who wears a hand-me-down hat and purse with expensive labels, and lights her cigarettes with Stork Club matches. Sitting alone in the kitchen, they talk completely at cross purposes, Mrs. Snell concerned about cooling her tea and missing her bus, and the hateful Sandra concerned only lest Lionel relay her slanderous words to Mrs. Tannenbaum. And there is a pathetic failure of communication between Boo Boo Tannenbaum, good as her intentions are, and her son, who in lonely isolation forbids her entry into the sailless boat in which he sits, impervious to her alternate cuteness, cajolery, and "just-us-men" approach. She is a plain, slight, not particularly feminine 25-year-old who, one suspects, is only a little better equipped to meet the Sandras of this world than is her son. (Walking to the dinghy she whistles "Kentucky Babe.") And one knows too that the efficacy of the kind of palliative she proffers—a jar of pickles and a boat ride with Daddy, and the pretense that a "kike" is "one of those things that go up in the *air*"—may not retain its potency much beyond Indian Summer.

## 6. "The Catcher in the Rye" (1951)

After "Down at the Dinghy" comes "For Esmé" and after "For Esmé" comes Salinger's most sustained success, *The Catcher in the Rye*. This novel's exciting resemblances to *The Adventures of*

*Huckleberry Finn* have been justly noted by a number of critics—the comic irony, the colloquial language, the picaresque structure, and the theme of anti-phoniness—and it is not inconceivable that some day Holden Caulfield may be as well known an American boy as Huck Finn. For a reader goes through much the same pattern of relishing both boys: first it is the release provided by their rebellion against society, then the inspiration of their honesty against sham, and then the sympathetic awareness of their melancholy roles. After the reader recovers from the releasing joy of Holden's invective (e.g., "Her son was doubtless the biggest bastard that ever went to Pencey, in the whole crumby history of the school") and of his exposure of phoniness (e.g., a Radio City Christmas complete with what has been identified as the movie of James Hilton's *Random Harvest*), he goes on to appreciate the pathos of Holden's loneliness and frustration.

But nervous cynicism and neurosis are not enough for fiction in depth, and the next step for a reader should be to realize that Holden Caulfield is actually a saintly Christian person (there is no need to call him a Christ-figure). True, he has little notion of the love of God, and he thinks that "all the children in our family are atheists." But (1) he himself never does a wrong thing: instead of commandments, Holden breaks only garage windows (when his brother dies) and the no-smoking rule in the Pencey dormitory. (2) He sacrifices himself in a constant war against evil, even though he has a poignantly Manichean awareness of its ubiquity ("If you had a million years to do it in, you couldn't rub out even *half* the [ubiquitously scrawled dirty words] in the world.") And most importantly, (3) his reward is

29

to understand that if one considers humanity, one must love it. The text for Holden's behavior is his insistence—oddly enough, to his Quaker friend Childs on absolute primitive Christianity: "Jesus never sent old Judas to Hell. . . . I think any one of the Disciples would've sent him to Hell and all—and fast, too—but I'll bet anything Jesus didn't do it."

For Jesus and Holden Caulfield truly love their neighbors, especially the poor in goods, appearance, and spirit. Holden not only gives ten dollars to the nuns in the station but also he is depressed by their meagre breakfast and the fact that they will never be "going anywhere swanky for lunch." He worries about where the ducks in Central Park can go when the water freezes, and how wretched his mother would feel if he died—"because she still isn't over my brother Allie yet." He is kind to the repulsive Ackley, with his "Sinus trouble, pimples, lousy teeth, halitosis, crumby fingernails," and he tries to obviate Slagle's envy of his Mark Cross luggage. Most significantly, for an adolescent undergoing the torturing growing pains of sex, he sympathizes with the girl's situation—with the ugly daughter of Pencey's headmaster, with both the ugly girl and the beautiful girl in the nightclub undergoing male treatment from their escorts, with the prostitute Sunny, with the girl whom Luce has enjoyed and now derogates, and especially with Jane Gallagher, the girl whose fear Holden appreciates (she wouldn't move her checker kings out of the back row) and whose virtue he fears Stradlater has taken. And like his Jesus with his Judas, he still forgives Stradlater and the bellboy Maurice who have betrayed and beaten him. Indeed, this is the old-fashioned moral, stated haltingly at the very end by Holden Caulfield, who wishes to be the Catcher in the Rye suffering little children to come to him and be saved from falling over the cliff. He puts it this way: "About all I know is, I sort of *miss* everybody I told you about. Even old Stradlater and Ackley, for instance. I think I even miss that goddam Maurice. It's funny. Don't ever tell anybody anything. If you do, you start missing everybody." In less concrete words: If you are aware of the human comedy, you must love individual human beings.[3] The ending of *The Catcher in the Rye* is just as artistically weak—and as humanly satisfying—as that of *Huckleberry Finn*.

# IV. SEEN THROUGH THE GLASS FAMILY, DARKLY:

*Religion through Satire*

After *The Catcher in the Rye* climaxed the great period of 1948-1951, Salinger brought out one more *New Yorker* story, in the same month that the novel appeared, and then published nothing for two years. The story, "Pretty Mouth and Green My Eyes," is a brief *tour de force* dialogue of marital infidelity perilously close to the dialect and promiscuity of O'Hara and the brummagem snappy ending of O. Henry. (Arthur, in bed with Lee's wife, listens on the phone to Lee's puzzled complaint of Joan's absence; Lee's second call is a pathetic lie that Joan has returned and all is well.)

But in 1953 the writer began to mine a new vein which the five stories published thereafter have not yet exhausted, even though the last two have exhausted some of the writer's admirers. These tales are "De Daumier-Smith's Blue Period" (first printed in *Nine Stories* but, according to its position there, written before "Teddy") and "Teddy," plus the three long, uncollected, and possibly unfinished stories about the Glass Family— "Franny," "Raise High the Roof Beam, Carpenters," and "Zooey." If Salinger continues on the track laid down in these tales, and manages to get back to the compression and tempo of the first three of them, he will make an overwhelmingly impressive contribution to modern writing. For the problem he has set himself in this last period is no less than the utilization of transcendental mysticism in satiric fiction, something (as far as we know) never attempted before by an American writer, and by only a few in Western literature.

De Daumier-Smith and Teddy McArdle, the protagonists in the last two of the *Nine Stories*, are notably different from the other central figures in the collection. De Daumier-Smith reveals himself as at once "a student of Buddhism," "an agnostic," "an admirer of St. Francis of Assisi," a man "especially delighted with Martin Luther," who falls in love with a painting of Christ's burial by a Roman Catholic nun, and who has a "transcendent" mystical experience. Teddy, the only completely good, completely adjusted, completely mature human being in the entire span of Salinger's serious work, is a child wonder who subscribes to Hindu doctrines. Franny, Zooey, Buddy and the Seymour Glass retrospectively seen in the later stories are half-Jewish, half-Irish prodigies brought up on comparative religions, especially Eastern. In short, Salinger has begun to make use of historical persons and doctrines to broaden and deepen his fiction. In doing so, he has retained the sardonic style, but in his last two stories he has allowed the spiritual content to overflow the style and drown all.

## 1. "De Daumier-Smith's Blue Period" (1953)

Salinger is in fine control in this fantastic and subtle tale, a humorous treatment of the classic Oedipal situation, wherein redirection of love to a conventional object is surprisingly achieved by means of religious impulse. The narrator's attitude towards his stepfather throughout childhood and adolescence is one of ill-concealed hostility. The strength of his feeling for his mother is made clear in his glib fantasy of a job-application letter ("I said I had just left my small estate in the South of France, following the death of my wife") and in a retrospective comment in another letter ("The happiest day of my life was many years ago when I was seventeen. I was on my way for lunch to meet my mother, who was going out on the street for the first time after a long illness.") Shortly after he finally articulates the nature of the situation with his stepfather ("we gradually discovered that we were both in love with the same deceased woman"), he leaves his rival's shelter and support.

Not only is there the representation of love for the mother with its repressed sexual component, but there are also repeated symptoms of father-hatred, even to the point of some unobtrusive castration imagery. The narrator thinks he has found escape and fulfillment when, under the name of Jean de Daumier-Smith, he secures a job as an instructor in a Montreal correspondence art school, Les Amis des Vieux Maitres, but it develops that he has only tossed himself into another family situation. The sole instructor-proprietors of the art school are Monsieur Yoshoto, a small man who barely speaks to the narrator, and Madame Yoshoto, taller and more attractive, who inspires his affection and shows some concern about his wishes, asking him on two occasions if he would prefer an egg to the fish she serves. Furthermore, he occupies the room of the Yoshotos' absent son.

Before the appearance of the third father-figure,

the narrator encounters by correspondence the force and the experience which will liberate him and resolve the problem of his psychological development. One of the pupils who falls to his lot is a Sister Irma of the Order of St. Joseph (still another father reference). Her painting technique is amateurish, but she has a remarkable talent. De Daumier-Smith immediately falls in love with her; and it is this love for a sweet and good woman (she teaches art and cooking to classes of "kittys") that permits him to make the transition from the Oedipal phase of the story's beginning to the normal and nearly adult heterosexual plane of the story's end. He lies awake thinking of her: "I tried to visualize the day I would visit her at her convent. I saw her coming to meet me—near a high-wire fence—a shy beautiful girl of eighteen who had not yet taken her final vows and was still free to go out into the world with the Peter Abelard-type man of her choice." Since she is, despite the age he specifies, essentially a mother-image, he must minimize the sexual side of his feeling: "I saw us walking slowly, silently, toward a far, verdant part of the convent grounds, where suddenly, and without sin, I would put my arm around her waist."

De Daumier-Smith's wildly emotional letter to Sister Irma, a desperate attempt to communicate with another sensitive spirit, as well as a covert but transparent declaration of love, results in the withdrawal of Sister Irma from the art course. But it is not Sister Irma who severs the relationship; it is Father Zimmerman, who has already registered forcibly in de Daumier-Smith's mind in a connection that suggests castration, his name being that of the dentist who had pulled out eight of his teeth. This recollection is very close to the sketch de Daumier-Smith had done earlier, on an easel set between his and his stepfather's twin beds, which showed "a cavernous view of the mouth of a man being attended by his dentist. The man's tongue is a simple, U. S. Treasury hundred dollar bill, and the dentist is saying, sadly, in French, 'I think we can save the molar, but I'm afraid that tongue will have to come out.' It was an enormous favorite of mine." One may also note here another castration image set forth in a letter from the protagonist to Sister Irma: "as I was coming into the Avenue Victor Hugo, which is a street in Paris, I bumped into a chap without any nose. I ask you to please consider that factor, in fact I beg you. It is quite pregnant with meaning." (The student of Salinger may also be reminded of the Laughing Man, the noseless monster originally created by Hugo in *L'Homme Qui Rit*.)

It is at this point that the reader may appreciate fully the richness of an earlier reference of de Daumier-Smith's. By calling himself a "Peter Abelard-type man," the youth identifies himself both as what he would like to be—a popular academic teacher, a philosopher, and a successful lover—and what his fantasies reveal him actually to be psychologically—a suffering castrate. Like Abelard with Eloise, further, he is a monk ("I live like an evil-minded monk," he writes Sister Irma) who falls in love with a pupil (Eloise entered a convent *after* the event) and who is punished for it by her protector, Irma's Father Zimmerman and Eloise's Canon Hulbert both being instruments of emasculation.

The resolution of all this chaos comes about when de Daumier-Smith, reacting against the loss of Sister Irma as a pupil, successively experiences the mystic's dark night of the soul and then an illumination. His concerns with religion, possibly quite as strong and demanding as those with sexual and psychological maturation, have already been indicated by his identification of himself as an agnostic acquainted with Buddhism, Roman Catholicism, and Protestantism. His art school is directly above an orthopedic appliances shop (he is psychologically crippled as we first see him), and it is while gazing into the windows of the shop that he experiences both phases in his religious progress. In the first phase, his fantasy represents him as a non-believer witnessing the Crucifixion of Christ: "The thought was forced on me that no matter how coolly or sensibly or gracefully I might one day learn to live my life, I would always at best be a visitor in a garden of enamel urinals and bedpans, with a sightless, wooden dummy-deity standing by in a marked down rupture truss." In the second phase ("my Experience"), a girl removing the truss from the dummy does a comic pratfall, but "Suddenly (and I say this, I believe, with all due self-consciousness), the sun came up and sped toward the bridge of my nose at the rate of ninety-three million miles a second. Blinded and very frightened—I had to put my hand on the glass to keep my balance. The thing lasted for no more than a few seconds. When I got my sight back, the girl had gone from the window, leaving behind her a shimmering field of exquisite, twice blessed enamel flowers." It is then that de Daumier-Smith, released by his love and his Experience, writes in his diary, "I am giving Sister Irma her freedom to follow her own destiny. Everybody is a nun." More than a statement of release, it is also a declaration of his own independence from the pure image he has subconsciously tried to preserve of his mother. The last sentence is, moreover, a profound if cryptic attempt to summarize the whole human condition: every human being, the boy seems to be saying, is cut off from others in one respect, yet has in him or her the possibilities of spiritual achievement, and it is sin for another human being to jeopardize those possibilities by making purely personal demands on him or her.

Both the ending and the beginning of "De Daumier-Smith's Blue Period" affirm the fact of the narrator's belated maturation. For a nineteen-year-old, the normalcy of the pursuit that occupies him after his resignation from the staff of Les Amis des Vieux Maitres is patent: "I packed up and joined Bobby, my stepfather, in Rhode Island, where I spent the next six or eight weeks, till art school reopened, investigating that most interesting of all summer-active animals, the American Girl in Shorts." Nor is this all. The very telling of the story (we are forcefully informed in its very first paragraph) is in itself a mature act demonstrating his release from jealousy of his stepfather. Bobby, says de Daumier-Smith, "was an adventurous, extremely magnetic, and generous man. (After having spent so many years laboriously begrudging him those picaresque [sic] adjectives, I feel it's a matter of life and death to get them in here.)"

The explication above does not by any means exhaust the subtleties and nuances of this ingenious story. The imagery that reinforces the basic theme is much more pervasive than indicated. For example, in contrast to Sister Irma and her work, de Daumier-Smith's other students and their efforts are completely secular and highly sexual. A young housewife with the pseudonym of Bambi Kramer has enclosed a photograph of herself in a strapless bathing-suit and has submitted a picture of "three small boys fishing in an odd-looking body of water, one of their jackets draped over a 'No Fishing!' sign." Another student's submissions include one that "satirized the familiar, everyday tragedy of a chaste young girl, with below-shoulder length blond hair and udder-sized breasts, being criminally assaulted in church, in the very shadow of the altar, by her minister. Both subjects' clothes were graphically in disarray." A completely nameless man sends a landscape dominated by "a forest of phallic symbols."

Another facet of this story is the subtlety with which it dramatizes the isolation suffered by de Daumier-Smith. The *cul de sacs* are Kafkaesque. We never learn the narrator's real name and he never learns the real names of three of his four students, one of whom is a woman with the name of a male deer. He has gone to Canada with a bogus identity and a false background to teach in a correspondence school bearing a French name and run by two Japanese whose name is not even a legitimate Japanese cognomen. M. Yoshoto never responds to the protagonist's compulsive conversational attempts, and other efforts to bridge the gap are just as futile: after ingratiatingly revealing that he is a student of Buddhism, de Daumier-Smith learns that the Yoshotos are Presbyterians. Every night he hears "A high, thin, broken moan" from behind their wall. "I never did find out which of the Yoshotos it came from," he says, "let alone why." Laboring in the instructors' room of the Les Amis slum tenement, he is isolated from his students (all but Sister Irma) quite as much by their failure of senstivity as by the physical distance that separates them. And when he releases Sister Irma with the words *"Tout le monde est une nonne,"* he means partly that everyone, in his aloneness, is like a nun cloistered from the normal contact of humanity.

Even the title bears on the progress from conflict to resolution in the tale. De Daumier-Smith, like the Picasso he claims to know as a family friend, proceeds through the Blue Period of melancholy concern with unfortunate *isolatoes.* But it is merely a period, and de Daumier-Smith, through Sister Irma, comes out of it to chase the American Girl in Shorts. As the story stands, it can hardly escape the label *tour de force,* but if only the protagonist were less precocious and the Yoshoto sequence less fantastic, the tale might take its place with "For Esmé," with love again resolving "squalor."

## 2. "Teddy" (1953)

The next story is another original idea—the rendering of unexpected mysticism, transcendentalism, and Korzybskian General Semantics vs. selfishness, mortality, and Aristotelian logic—and it is marred only by a growing diffuseness and by the referents of the story's last two sentences. The diffuseness, which comes in the conversation between the mortally curious Nicholson, the confidant of the story, and the immortally composed Teddy, does not really get out of hand, but it hints at the interminable Glass Family discussions to come. In the confusion at the end of the tale, Nicholson hears a scream "clearly coming from a small, female child. It was highly acoustical, as though it were reverberating within four tiled walls." Since Teddy McArdle (aged ten) was to meet his sister Booper (aged six) at the Atlantic liner's swimming-pool at this time, the scream must come from Booper. But the acousticality seems to place Booper either simply in the room surrounding the pool, which is often tiled, or in the pool, emptied, itself—and we have heard Teddy tell Nicholson how the pool might be empty today, leading us to the possibility that Booper screams as she falls into the waterless pool. But Teddy had also conjectured that his sister might push him in, killing him instantly, and since he has made a solipsistic farewell to his parents early in the story ("After I go out this door, I may only exist in the minds of all my acquaintances"), and has written in his diary "It will either happen today or February 14, 1958," and has quoted to Nicholson a Japanese poem "Nothing in the voice of the cicada intimates how soon it will die," we can only conclude that Booper, already rendered as a sadistic child, pushes Teddy in and then screams as he is killed by the fall. But there is no discernible reason for the temporary ambiguity,[4] especially as Salinger had already demonstrated in "A Perfect Day for Bananafish" his ability to make a straightforward account of death climactic and necessary.

At any rate, the figure of Teddy is memorable and even inspirational. As a child prodigy who is not only more astute than his shouting radio-actor father and nicer than his indulgent sardonic mother, but who understands them and forgives them, he is the acme of all the selfless love evidenced in such varying degrees by the youthful Ginnie Mannox, Esmé, Jean de Daumier-Smith, and Holden Caulfield. Teddy loves God but not sentimentally, and he also *accepts* humanity—his stupid parents, his curious doctors, and his hating, hateful sister—knowing that things are what they are and that living and dying are neither good nor evil. He is a mystic who receives his inevitable death with a spiritual equanimity that contrasts starkly with the logical and emotional egocentricity of everybody else in the story.

### 3. Zen Buddhism and the Glass Menagerie

With this concluding achievement in mind, the reader can go back and work on the epigraph to *Nine Stories:*

*We know the sound of two hands clapping.*
*But what is the sound of one hand clapping?*

To the merely literary, this might appear comic, possibly some echo of the Krishna ceremony in Forster's *A Passage to India,* where the Hindu Godbole lays down one cymbal so that he can adjust his pince-nez, while with the other cymbal he clashes the air. To the merely critical, the saying might stimulate symbolic application to the stories, with something made of the isolation, the "one hand clapping," of Seymour, Eloise, and so many others. But students of comparative religion would recognize this as the most famous of the 1700-odd *koans* of Zen Buddhism, those surrealistic unanswerable conundrums designed to stir up and readjust one's view of things. "Zen has always specialized in nonsense," Aldous Huxley puts it, "as a means of stimulating the mind to go forward to that which is beyond sense. . . ." A *koan* thus makes a perfect epigraph for a writer who wishes to entitle his book of nine stories *Nine Stories:* the reader has not to apply the quotation *to* the tales but simply to be thereby aware that the tales present problems which he may or may not solve for himself by suprasensory perception.

Yet the background of the *koans* may be explored here a little more, since it provides a clue to what the characters in Salinger's most recent stories are in conflict with and what they are seeking. Zen Buddhism, even according to its adepts, is as impossible to define and describe as any transcendentalism. It is not a religion, not a philosophy, not an ethic, and not even a psychology (though to a Westerner it certainly sounds like all these), but a Way, an attitude with intuitive spiritual enlightenment as its goal. ". . . Zen is above all an experience, nonverbal in character," says Alan Watts, "which is simply inaccessible to the purely literary and scholarly approach. To know what Zen is, and especially what it is not, there is no alternative but to practice it. . . ."

For readers of the Glass Family saga, possibly the most helpful comments on Zen are two by its most famous explicator in the West, Professor Daisetz Suzuki of Columbia, whose work is said to have stimulated Salinger. (1) "The basic idea of Zen is to come in touch with the inner workings of our being, and to do this in the most direct way possible, without resorting to anything external or superadded." (2) "As I conceive it, Zen is the ultimate fact of all philosophy and religion. . . . Therefore Zen is not necessarily the fountain of Buddhist thought and life alone; it is very much alive also in Christianity, Mohammedanism, in Taoism, and even in positivistic Confucianism. . . . Zen is what makes the religious feeling run through its legitimate channel and what gives life to the intellect."

What Seymour, Zooey, and Franny Glass seem to want to do is "to come in touch with the inner workings" of their beings, to achieve non-intellectual enlightenment—what Zen Buddhists call *satori*, "to be in a state of pure consciousness" (this is Buddy Glass quoting Dr. Suzuki) that "is to be with God before he said, Let there be light." With all religions at their fingertips, the Glass siblings utilize anything Zen-like, and it is their comparative success or failure in this enterprise that forms the basic conflicts of their stories. Furthermore, the farther away from this conflict a story gets, the more unsuccessful it is as a work of art.

To understand the relationship of the Glasses to Zen, we must first be aware of the blood relationship of the Glasses to each other, a pattern remotely reminiscent of *Abie's Irish Rose*. The parents are an old Pantages Circuit vaudeville team, Les and Bessie Glass, which fact, since Les is Jewish and Bessie an Irish girl named Gallagher, calls up the old team of Gallagher and Shean (Schoenberg).[5] As vaudevillians, the Glass parents are not such a complete contrast as one might expect to their seven children, five brothers and two sisters, most of whom begin life as child prodigies on a radio quiz program and end up as monologuists of the psyche. (One cannot resist noting that Al Shean was uncle to the five Marx Brothers.) Seymour (1917-1948) is the oldest, the wisest (though not because of his Ph.D.), and the most psychotic: he is of course the one who committed suicide in "A Perfect Day for Bananafish." Buddy is a writer, as shy and as sardonic as Seymour, but unmarried and vaguely maladjusted at the age of 38. Then comes Boo Boo, wife of Tannenbaum and mother of Lionel (and two more) in "Down at the Dinghy," who has so far shown more wit than Zen, and who—*pace* Marjorie Morningstar!— prefers to be described in "Zooey" as "a Tuckahoe homemaker." The twins, Walt and Waker, are next, characterized chiefly by Waker's being labeled a Roman Catholic priest and Walt's being introduced in "Uncle Wiggily in Connecticut" as Eloise's humorous fiancé who was killed in 1945. Zachary Martin Glass, the sixth child, known as Zooey, is a TV actor in his late twenties with an ulcer and the adolescent arrogance of Franklin Graff in "Just before the War with the Eskimos." Franny, currently at college, is the youngest and most attractive, physically and emotionally, of this Glass menagerie.

## 4. "Raise High the Roof Beam, Carpenters" (1955)

The telling of this long anecdote is a devotional act of Buddy toward his beloved brother Seymour, and it may also be Salinger's compulsive attempt to explain why Seymour killed himself in "A Perfect Day for Bananafish." Setting forth the circumstances of the marriage to Muriel Fedder in 1942, it reveals Seymour's sensitivity and neuroticism, which may doom the marriage. The frame for the events of the late May wedding is the microscopic account by Buddy of how he got a furlough, got to the wedding, and defended his brother and himself against the onslaughts of the Matron of Honor, a self-righteous belligerent young woman who is incensed at Seymour's failure to appear for the wedding. Somewhere in this interminable yarn, Buddy locks himself in the bathroom to read excerpts from Seymour's 1941-1942 diary, which reveal that Seymour's trouble is spirituality and euphoria rather than the schizophrenia and latent homosexuality diagnosed by the crass Matron of Honor. Seymour, describing himself as "too *happy* to get married," confesses, "Oh, God, if I'm anything by a clinical name, I'm a kind of paranoid in reverse. I suspect people of plotting to make me happy." The crazy conflict between Buddy and the Matron of Honor is resolved by the late intelligence that Seymour has returned to elope with Muriel.

The point of the 16,000-word tale, imbedded in what sometimes resembles an eye's investigation of itself in a mirror, seems to be that Seymour, who has achieved the *satori* of Zen, is thereby considered abnormal by the world and is loved only by his siblings. (It is Boo Boo who writes on Seymour's bathroom mirror the somewhat pointed Sapphic epithalamion—in the literal Wharton translation beloved by the Glasses—"Raise high the roof beam, carpenters. Like Ares comes the bridegroom, taller far than a tall man.") But this point is almost completely obscured by the mass of detail which Salinger introduces into the long scenes in the taxi and in Buddy's apartment, by the false leads he allows to stand, and by the irrelevant characterization of a Mrs. Silsburn, a Lieutenant Burwick, and a deaf-mute uncle of the bride's father. Seymour is offstage during the entire "drama," and the diary-and-letter method of narration, no matter how insightful, is not adequate compensation—not to mention the lame introduction of the all-important diary: "I decided to take it into the bathroom and read parts of it and *then* drop it into the laundry hamper."

## 5. "Franny" (1955)

It is quite another story with "Franny," the best chapter in the Glass history largely because it is the shortest (10,000 words) and the most concentrated. Franny is a guest of Lane Coutell at an Ivy League football weekend in 1954, and preoccupied not with revelry but with religion. She tries to love Lane, but he is too concerned with himself, and she finds her own college teachers and friends and herself too self-centered to generate love. "I'm just sick of ego, ego, ego," she mourns. "My own and everybody else's. I'm sick of everybody that wants to *get* somewhere, do something distinguished and all, be somebody interesting. It's disgusting—it is, it *is*."

Franny's only support in this crisis is a little devotional book, *The Way of a Pilgrim*, which focuses on a simple prayer to compose spiritual unrest: "Lord Jesus Christ, have mercy on me." Franny finally admits to Lane that "if you keep saying that prayer over and over again—you only have to do it with your *lips* at first—then eventually what happens, the prayer becomes self-active." After she has fainted and been revived, the story ends with her lips soundlessly moving, presumably a signal that she is at least striving toward some remote *satori*.

Surprisingly enough, this tale works out quite well, what with the concentration on one Glass all the way through—an attractive 21-year-old girl sincerely upset by the egocentrism of the world that has engulfed her, awkwardly struggling and partially succeeding in finding some spiritual sustenance even if it ruins her "normal" role in a conventional boy-girl situation. (One must reject even while one understands the specious reading of the story, apparently widespread in certain colleges, that made "Franny" a study of an emotional and physical reaction to an illicit pregnancy.) The atmosphere and dialogue seem authentic and representative, and the human agent in Franny's conflict—the sophisticated campus intellectual with his "I mean, hell" and concern with his wonderful paper on Flaubert—is a satisfying object of both satire and sympathy. One

47

may feel that this is a story belonging in Salinger's 1948-1951 period. Indeed, the youthful contretemps between Franny and Lane has some reversed relevance to the "slight rebellion off Madison" between Holden Caulfield and Sally Hayes, and the chicken sandwich scorned by Lane and untouched by Franny calls up the symbolic chicken sandwich of "Just before the War with the Eskimos" which Franklin offers and which Ginnie finally accepts in a gesture of charitable love.

## 6. "Zooey" (1957)

"Zooey," published two-and-a-half years after "Franny," with "Raise High the Roof Beam, Carpenters," in between, is the sequel on the Monday following Franny's partial breakdown and return to the Glass home in New York. One may guess—without caring to check the fact—that "Zooey" must be the longest (29,000 words) and dullest "short story" ever to appear in *The New Yorker* in its thirty years of surprises. Any reader who gets through it and happens to turn back a hundred pages to the opening will agree heartily with the narrator (Buddy again) that the piece "isn't really a short story at all but a sort of prose home movie," and with "those who have seen the footage" who "have strongly advised me against nurturing any elaborate distribution plans for it." If Salinger is currently putting together a novel about the Glasses, one hopes that "Zooey" will undergo the same shaping consideration that the author gave to his first Caulfield family stories when he came to write *The Catcher in the Rye*.

For "Zooey" has eight undesignated parts to it —two or three of which might have served by themselves to advance the case history of Franny and/or the Glasses; as they stand, none is in happy proportion to one another or to the whole. Part 1 is a totally unnecessary first-person introduction by Buddy Glass, whose stylistic master is S. J. Perelman. Buddy then disappears as narrator, but Part 2, which describes Zooey and the Glass family in un-Perelmanian terms (including a long footnote) is merely a prelude to Part 3, which consists of "an almost endless-looking letter" from Buddy to Zooey on the third anniversary of Seymour's suicide. Zooey is sitting in the Glass bathtub reading the letter (which exhorts him to *Act with all your might*) six years after it was written. (Could there be any significance in the fact that one of the links among these last three Salinger stories is the fact that in "Roof Beam" Buddy reads Seymour's diary in the bathroom, in "Zooey" Zooey reads Buddy's letter in the bathroom, and in "Franny" Franny reads *The Way of a Pilgrim* in a ladies room? An answer might be that it signifies the family shyness carried to an extreme in Seymour's agoraphobia.) Part 4, also laid in the bathroom, is a prolix *causerie* between Zooey and his mother that serves only to characterize Zooey and his mother—something the classic Salinger could have done in a phrase (e.g. "my wife, a breathtakingly level-headed girl," or " 'Poor Uncle Wiggily' "). Part 5 at least gets Zooey out of the bathroom and into the living-room, where he and Franny converse, also at length. This is where the story should have begun, for herein Franny and her arrogant brother touch on not only Franny's crisis but Zooey's, both of which, in terms of their education by Seymour and Buddy, could be described as the dark night of the soul. In Part 6, which also could have been condensed and utilized in a good story, Zooey cruelly lectures his sister on her having a wrong attitude to the Jesus Prayer: she is having "a tenth-rate nervous breakdown" because she is not really saying the prayer to Jesus but to herself, and "This is *God's* universe, buddy, not yours. . . ." But the basic conflict is once again interrupted by Part 7 while Zooey enters and examines the room formerly occupied by Seymour and Buddy; untenanted for seven years, it still contains Seymour's listed telephone. In Part 8 Zooey calls up Franny on this phone and pretends to be Buddy, but when exposed, reverts to his lecture on Franny's self-interest.

Here, however, he begins to make some sense, and in the conclusion—which the magazine reader may have suspected was coming only in a later issue—he neatly resolves the conflict of what could have been a good episode in Franny's spiritual progress. He reminds Franny of how Seymour used to make them shine their shoes before the radio quiz program. Why? For the Fat Lady out there, in the audience whose sordid life he left them to envision. All right; Franny is forgetting that the people whom she finds spiritually frustrating are all Seymour's Fat Lady. "There isn't anyone anywhere that isn't Seymour's Fat Lady. Don't you know that? Don't you know that goddam secret yet? And don't you know—*listen* to me, now—*don't you know who that Fat Lady really is?* . . . Ah, buddy, Ah, buddy. It's Christ Himself. Christ Himself, buddy." The effect of Zooey's dramatic sincerity is to give Franny "joy" (i.e., *satori*) and to allow her to fall into a deep sleep.

Salinger has said something morally profound here, but hardly esthetically original. Zooey's first secret, that everyone is Seymour's Fat Lady, is merely a Broadway version of Christ's second commandment, already exemplarily embodied in Holden Caulfield: Thou shalt love thy neighbor as thyself. Something very much like his second secret has already served as the revelation ending the Blue Period of Jean de Daumier-Smith: "Everybody is a nun." Furthermore, the end of this saga is one Salinger had already brilliantly utilized for his best story: Esmé's gesture of love, like Zooey's, enabled Sergeant X, like Franny, to go to sleep, and "You take a really sleepy man, Esmé, and he *always* stands a chance of again becoming a man with all his fac—with all his f-a-c-u-l-t-i-e-s intact." For Salinger, it would seem, the dark night of the soul is not quite Scott Fitzgerald's three o'clock in the morning, but the symptom of its end is sleep.

Buddy quotes Fitzgerald's Nick Carraway at the beginning of "Zooey," going on to say that his own cardinal virtue is to "know the difference between a mystical story and a love story. I say that my current offering isn't a mystical story, or a religiously mystifying story, at all. *I* say that's it's a compound, or multiple, love story, pure and complicated." And it is a multiple love story in the sense that several kinds of love—spiritual, universal, and familial (sexual love is notably absent in the Glass house) are discussed and occasionally displayed. But once again Salinger's fine eye for the insignificant detail has dissolved a promising multiple love story into the very "prose home movie" that Buddy also labels it. As a dramatic director, Buddy-Salinger is most often "a regular Belasco," loading the stage with real snow for Setting, or bringing out Character according to the Contents-of-Small-Boy's-Pockets School—as with the lists of what Mother Glass's kimono pockets

51

contain (ten items), what the Glass medicine cabinet contains (fifty-five items, plus "quite a good deal more"), what the Glass livingroom contains (more than four dozen items, not to mention eight titles of books in the bookcases), plus twelve quotations, given in full, out of the twenty-dozen odd inscribed on the door of Seymour's room. Indeed, the home movie is just what the masked Buddy describes his own letter to Zooey as being: "virtually endless in length, overwritten, teaching, repetitious, opinionated, remonstrative, condescending, embarrassing," even if it is also "filled to a surfeit, with affection." As with "For Esmé," there is love and squalor, but it is the verbiage rather than the human condition that is squalid here.

# V. CONCLUSION
## *The Way of a Pilgrim*

We end as we began, noting that J. D. Salinger is the contemporary American writer of fiction most popular with the younger generation, and that it is well to discover just what is good and what is bad about his work. His career has not been that of a Hemingway or a Wolfe or a Fitzgerald of the last generation—writers who from the very beginning produced successful fiction embodying their major themes and techniques. Salinger's career—one discovers on examination—has been a slowly maturing and then suddenly bloating process: it was bogged down in trivial magazine tales for a half-dozen years, was apparently released by the experience of World War II, came to a height with a half-dozen stories and a novel in the 1948-1951 period, and has been declining recently as its noble attempt to adapt a habitual satiric style to almost purely religious themes has become self-conscious.

On the one hand, we have in his *corpus* a series of great fictional symbols and events—the Goebbels-Dostoevsky juxtaposition in "For Esmé," Holden Caulfield eternally rubbing out eternally dirty words from the walls of the world, the swollen bananafish of doom, poor Uncle Wiggily, the tragic death of the Laughing Man and the pa-

53

thetic death of Teddy, Franny's agonized praying, the brilliant religious resolution of the sexual problems of Jean de Daumier-Smith. These constructs differ notably from—even as they far outweigh—the unsteady point of view and tone of so many of the tales like "The Inverted Forest," or Zooey's bathroom lecture.

Admirers of this writer are, of course, entitled to worry a little. J. D. Salinger learned too long ago that everyone in the world is Seymour's Fat Lady, just as he learned and then forgot that an artist can make use of depth psychology without retailing every item of a case history. Whatever is going on right now with the Glass Family evidences a curious esthetic amnesia in the realm of these basic discoveries, and the sympathetic reader can only hope that all is not lost. Or he may find himself involuntarily crying out, in Zooey's accents: "Ah, buddy. Ah, buddy. Can't you get *off* this turntable? Fiction's a lot more than just *talk—you* know *that*. It's *ac*tion and *con*flict, buddy. And you can turn 'em out a*gain*, buddy, with one of those hands tied behind your *back*. The *other* hand is the one that makes the *clap*ping sound."

# VI. FOOTNOTES

1. Quoted by John Clellon Holmes, "The Philosophy of the Beat Generation," *Esquire*, XLIX (Feb. 1958), 35. Kerouac seems to be speaking as a member of Salinger's Glass Family when he goes on to say: " 'I pray to my little brother, who died, and to my father, and to Buddha, and to Jesus Christ, and to the Virgin Mary. I pray to those five *people* . . .' " (p. 38).

2. There is an interesting cluster of associations in Salinger's work progressing from Seymour's Rilke to Rilke's admiration of Picasso's *Les Saltimbanques*, the painting appropriately mentioned in Salinger's "De Daumier-Smith's Blue Period," and thence to Seymour's Glass Family, vaudevillians and public performers who bear some resemblance to Picasso's *saltimbanques* as described by Rilke in the Fifth Duino Elegy.

3. This brings up remarkable parallels between *The Catcher in the Rye* (1951) and William Saroyan's *The Human Comedy* (1943), whose boy protagonist expresses something very close to Holden's fumbling conclusion: "I don't know anybody to hate. Byfield knocked me down when I was running the low hurdles, but I can't hate *him*, even" (Stradlater and Maurice had knocked Holden down). There is an objectionable (for different reasons) boy named Ackley in each story, and there is a metrical and orthographical similarity between the names of the protagonists Holden Caulfield and Homer Macauley (and cf. "Byfield"). Holden (aged 16) and Homer (who passes for 16) each has a sister and two brothers with one of the brothers dead or dying. At Pencey Prep, Holden gets into trouble in a history course studying the Egyptians; at Ithaca High School, Homer gets into trouble in a history course studying the Assyrians; and there is some curious nose-imagery in both sequences. The student comic at Pencey is named Edgar Marsalla; at Ithaca, Joe Terranova. Holden and Homer

both undergo scenes with somebody else's mother and with prostitutes.

It is a measure of *The Catcher in the Rye's* superiority over *The Human Comedy* that although both protagonists love humanity, Saroyan's concept is embodied chiefly in moralistic statements rather than dramatic action, as when Homer's mother tells him, "You must give to all who come into your life."

4. Professor Charles Murrah sees no "temporary ambiguity" here: "The reader's *distance* from the final catastrophe is appropriate—even necessary—because of *his* distance from Teddy's mind. We know that Teddy is a genius and a clairvoyant mystic; we do not, however, really understand him. At the end of the story we know that his sister has killed him, but the details are not graphically rendered. The unattached, reverberating scream from a child out of sight strikes just the right note of mystery and horror, sounding from behind the barrier imposed by our limited cognizance."

5. Or possibly Dolly Levi—née Gallagher—the matchmaker of Thornton Wilder's *The Merchant of Yonkers* (1938).

# VII.  BIBLIOGRAPHY

## 1. A Check-List of J. D. Salinger's Fiction

1940  The Young Folks. *Story*, XVI (Mar.-Apr.), 26-30

1941  The Hang of It. *Collier's*, CVIII (12 July), 22
      The Heart of a Broken Story. *Esquire*, XVI (Sept.), 32, 131-133

1942  Personal Notes on an Infantryman. *Collier's*, CX (12 July), 96
      The Long Debut of Lois Taggett. *Story*, XXI (Sept.-Oct.), 28-34

1943  The Varioni Brothers. *Saturday Evening Post*, CCXVI (17 July), 12-13, 76-77

1944  Both Parties Concerned. *Saturday Evening Post*, CCXVI (26 Feb.), 14, 47-48
      Soft-Boiled Sergeant. *Saturday Evening Post*, CCXVI (15 Apr.), 18, 82, 84-85
      Last Day of the Last Furlough. *Saturday Evening Post*, CCXVII (15 July), 26-27, 61-62, 64
      Once a Week Won't Kill You. *Story*, XXV (Nov.-Dec.), 23-27

1945  A Boy in France. *Saturday Evening Post*, CCXVII (31 Mar.), 21, 92
      Elaine. *Story*, XXV (Mar.-Apr.), 38-47
      This Sandwich Has No Mayonnaise. *Esquire*, XXIV (Oct.), 54-56, 147-149
      The Stranger. *Collier's*, CXVI (1 Dec.), 18, 77
      I'm Crazy. *Collier's*, CXVI (22 Dec.), 36, 48, 51

1946 Slight Rebellion off Madison. *New Yorker,* XXII (21 Dec.), 82-86

1947 A Young Girl in 1941 with No Waist at All. *Mademoiselle* (May), 222-223, 292-302

The Inverted Forest. *Cosmopolitan,* CXIII (Dec.), 73-80, 85-86, 88, 90, 92, 95-96, 98, 100, 102, 104

1948 A Perfect Day for Bananafish. *New Yorker,* XXIII (31 Jan.), 21-25

A Girl I Knew. *Good Housekeeping,* CXXVI (Feb.), 36, 186, 188, 191-196

Uncle Wiggily in Connecticut. *New Yorker,* XXIV (20 Mar.), 30-36

Just before the War with the Eskimos. *New Yorker,* XXIV (5 June), 37-40

Blue Melody. *Cosmopolitan,* CXXV (Sept.), 51-51, 112-119

1949 The Laughing Man. *New Yorker,* XXV (19 March), 27-32

Down at the Dinghy. *Harper's,* CXCVIII (Apr.), 87-91

1950 For Esmé—with Love and Squalor. *New Yorker,* XXVI (8 Apr.), 28-36

1951 *The Catcher in the Rye,* Boston: Little, Brown

Pretty Mouth and Green My Eyes. *New Yorker,* XXVII (14 July), 20-24

1953 De Daumier-Smith's Blue Period. *Nine Stories,* Boston: Little, Brown

Teddy. *New Yorker,* XXVIII (31 Jan.), 26-34

1955 Franny. *New Yorker,* XXX (29 Jan.), 24-32

Raise High the Roof Beam, Carpenters. *New Yorker,* XXXI (19 Nov.), 51-58, 60, 62, 65-66, 68, 70, 72-74, 76, 78-80, 83-84, 86-92, 95-98, 100-105, 107-110

1957 Zooey. *New Yorker,* XXXIII (4 May), 32-42, 44, 47-48, 52, 54, 57-59, 62, 64, 67-68, 70, 73-74, 76-78, 83-84, 86-88, 91-94, 97-98, 100-104, 107-114, 117-135

1959 Seymour: An Introduction. *New Yorker,* XXXV
      ( 6 June ), 42-52, 54-111

1961 *Franny and Zooey,* Boston: Little, Brown

1963 *Raise High the Roof Beam, Carpenters* and *Seymour:*
      *An Introduction,* Boston: Little, Brown

1965 Hapworth 16, 1924. *New Yorker,* XLI ( 19 June ),
      32-40

## 2. Critical Studies of Salinger's Fiction

1954 Hugh Maclean, "Conservatism in Modern American
      Fiction," *College English,* XV (March), 315-325.

1956 Arthur Heiserman and James E. Miller, Jr., "J. D.
      Salinger: Some Crazy Cliff," *Western Humanities*
      *Review,* X (Spring), 129-137.

      James F. Matthews, "J. D. Salinger: An Appraisal,"
      *University of Virginia Magazine,* I (Spring), 52-60.

      Charles Kaplan, "Holden and Huck: The Odysseys
      of Youth," *College English,* XVIII (November),
      76-80.

1957 David L. Stevenson, "J. D. Salinger: The Mirror of
      Crisis," *Nation,* CLXXXIV (9 March), 215-217.

      Charles H. Kegel, "Incommunicability in Salinger,
      *The Catcher in the Rye,*" *Western Humanities*
      *Review,* XI ( Spring 1957 ), 188-190.

      Albert Fowler, "Alien in the Rye," *Modern Age,* I
      (Fall), 193-197.

      Stewart Dodge, "In Search of 'The Fat Lady'," *The*
      *English Record* (N. Y. State English Council),
      VIII (Winter), 10-13.

      Edgar Branch, "Mark Twain and J. D. Salinger: A
      Study in Literary Continuity," *American Quar-*
      *terly,* IX, No. 2, Part 1 (Summer), 144-158.

      Ihab H. Hassan, "Rare Quixotic Gesture: The Fic-
      tion of J. D. Salinger," *Western Review,* XXI
      (Summer), 261-280.

      Frederic I. Carpenter, "The Adolescent in American
      Fiction," *English Journal,* XLVI (September),
      313-319.

Donald Barr, "Saints, Pilgrims and Artists," *Commonweal*, LXVII (25 October), 88-90.

1958 William Wiegand, "J. D. Salinger: Seventy-Eight Bananas," *Chicago Review*, II (Winter), 3-19.

Martin Green, "Amis and Salinger: The Latitude of Private Conscience," *Chicago Review*, II (Winter), 20-25.

Maxwell Geismar, "J. D. Salinger: The Wise Child and the *New Yorker* School of Fiction," in *American Moderns: From Rebellion to Conformity*, New York: Hill and Wang, 195-209.

1959 Donald P. Costello, "The Language of *The Catcher in the Rye*," *American Speech*, XXXIV (October), 172-181.

Tom Davis, "J. D. Salinger: A Checklist," *Papers of the Bibliographical Society of America*, LIII, 69-71.

Granville Hicks, "J. D. Salinger: Search for Wisdom," *Saturday Review*, XLII (July 25), 13, 30.

Arthur Mizener, "The Love Song of J. D. Salinger," *Harpers*, CCXVIII (February), 83-90.

1960 Tom Davis, "J. D. Salinger: 'Some Crazy Cliff' Indeed," *Western Humanities Review*, XIV, 97-99.

1961 James E. Bryan, "J. D. Salinger: The Fat Lady and the Chicken Sandwich," *College English*, XXIII (December), 226-229.

Peter J. Seng, "The Fallen Idol: The Immature World of Holden Caulfield," *College English*, XXIII (December), 203-209.

Carl F. Strauch, "Kings in the Back Row: Meaning through Structure — A Reading of Salinger's *The Catcher in the Rye*," *Wisconsin Studies in Contemporary Literature*, II (Winter), 5-30.

1962 William F. Belcher, and James W. Lee, eds., *J. D. Salinger and the Critics*, Belmont, Calif.: Wadsworth.

James E. Bryan, "Salinger's Seymour's Suicide," *College English*, XXIV (December), 226-229.

Henry A. Grunwald, ed., *Salinger: A Critical and Personal Portrait*, New York: Harper & Row.

Paul Phillips, "Salinger's *Franny and Zooey*," *Mainstream*, XV, 32-39.

1963 Alfred Chester, "Salinger: How to Live Without Love," *Commentary*, XXXV (June), 467-474.

Donald P. Costello, "Salinger and His Critics," *Commonweal*, LXXIX (25 October), 132-135.

Warren French, *J. D. Salinger*, New York: Twayne.

Arthur F. Kinney, "J. D. Salinger and the Search for Love," *Texas Studies in Language and Literature*, V (Spring), 111-126.

Marvin Laser, and Norman Fruman, eds., *Studies in J. D. Salinger: Reviews, Essays, and Critiques of "The Catcher in the Rye" and Other Fiction*, New York: Odyssey.

Malcolm M. Marsden, *If You Really Want to Know: A "Catcher" Casebook*, Chicago: Scott-Foresman.

"Special Number: Salinger. [original] Articles by Ihab Hassan, Warren G. French, Carl F. Strauch, Sam S. Baskett, John O. Lyons, John Russell, Arthur Schwartz, Joseph Blotner, and a Salinger bibliography by Donald M. Fiene," *Wisconsin Studies in Contemporary Literature*, IV (Winter).

Kermit Vanderbilt, "Symbolic Resolution in *The Catcher in the Rye:* The Cap, the Carousel and the American West," *Western Humanities Review*, XVII (Summer), 271-277.

1964 Kenneth Hamilton, "J. D. Salinger's Happy Family," *Queen's Quarterly*, LXXI, 176-187.

——, "One Way to Use the Bible: The Example of J. D. Salinger," *Christian Scholar*, XLVII (Fall), 243-251.

Richard Lettis, ed., *J. D. Salinger: "The Catcher in the Rye,"* Woodbury, N.Y.: Barron's Educational Series.

J. D. O'Hara, "No Catcher in the Rye," *Modern Fiction Studies*, IX (Winter), 370-376.

1965 Lyle Glazier, "The Glass Family Saga: Argument and Epiphany," *College English*, XXVII (December), 248-251.

James E. Miller, Jr., *J. D. Salinger*, Minneapolis: U. of Minnesota Press.

William Wiegand, "Salinger and Kierkegaard," *Minnesota Review*, V (May-July), 137-156.

1966 David D. Galloway, "The Love Ethic," in *The Absurd Hero in American Fiction: Updike, Styron, Bellow, Salinger,* Austin: U. of Texas Press, 140-169; also, "A J. D. Salinger Checklist," 226-251.

"J. D. Salinger Special Number. Original articles by John Russell, Bernice and Sanford Goldstein, John Antico, Brother Fidelian Burke, John V. Hagopian, Hubert I. Cohen, John M. Howell, and 'Criticism of J. D. Salinger: A Selected Checklist,' by Maurice Beebe and Jennifer Sperry," *Modern Fiction Studies,* XII (Autumn).